# Warm Ups

## &

# Wind Downs:

## 101 Activities
## for Moving and
## Motivating Groups

by
**Sandra Peyser Hazouri**
and
**Miriam Smith McLaughlin**

ISBN 0-932-796-52-4

Library of Congress Catalog No. 93-70220

Current printing of this edition (last digit):

9   8   7   6   5

*Production editor—*
**Don L. Sorenson**

*Graphic design—*
**Earl R. Sorenson**

*Artwork—*
**Christine M. Brown**

## Dedication

To Belle and Ed—
A special Mom and Dad
SPH
To Aaron Wyman—
A very special boy
MSM

## This book will be useful for:

- Staff Development
- Classrooms
- Management Team Training
- Peer Helper Programs
- Teacher Training
- Team Building
- Clubs
- Support Groups
- Community Groups

# Table of Contents

# Activity Design

The activities in *Warm Ups & Wind Downs* are divided into broad categories for the convenience of the trainer. Many of the activities can effectively fit into some area other than that under which they are listed. For example there are several group building activities that would be effective closures.

The times noted beside each activity are estimates because the time an activity will take is directly related to the number of people involved. The more people, the longer the activity will take to do and to process. We have attempted to address this issue, too, by suggesting grouping for larger numbers of people. An activity can often involve large numbers if the participants are divided into small groups. For example, an activity involving personal sharing would require an unreasonable amount of time in a group of fifty. If, however, that sharing occurred in ten groups of five participants, the time commitment would become manageable. Some activities are not workable in small groups and those have been identified as well.

The materials needed for each activity are listed along with any preparation that should be done ahead of time. It is a good idea to have staple supplies such as newsprint, markers, tape, scissors, plain paper, and name tags always available.

Endings to activities in this book most often involve processing what occurred. The questions and reflections are suggestions. Leaders and trainers can devise their own processing questions that are specifically related to the topic of the workshop.

Perhaps the key to the success of any activity is the enthusiasm and comfort level of the leader. Do not choose to lead an activity in which you would feel uncomfortable participating. Model for your group by demonstrating the degree of sharing or risk taking you expect from them. If you enjoy yourself, your group will enjoy themselves as well.

Sandra Peyser Hazouri and Miriam Smith McLaughlin

# Chapter I
# Get Acquainted
# Activities

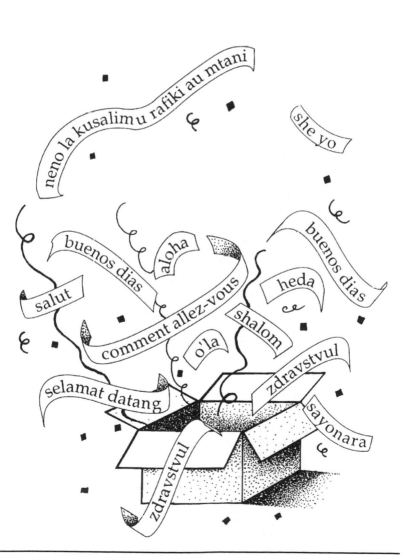

# Introduction

"No one is a part of the group until he or she speaks in the group." This quote, from a family therapist, is as true in educational and training settings as it is in the therapeutic arena. Speaking in the group can, of course, range from saying one's name to sharing some personal information with others. The intent is for people to begin developing a sense of security that will influence their willingness to participate and ask questions as the workshop or training progresses. Get acquainted activities should begin to move the group in that direction.

The kind of group and the time constraints of the program will determine the kind of get acquainted activity that might be appropriate for a particular group. Participants who will be together for only a few hours will need to spend considerably less time getting to know one another than those who will be together for days or weeks. A group of elementary school teachers would enjoy get acquainted activities that might not appeal to a group of computer programmers. A group of high school students and a group of middle school students are likely to respond differently to the same activity.

It is important to remember here, however, that activities that may seem childish or frivolous are often greatly enjoyed by adults. There is a child in all of us and most adults appreciate an opportunity now and then to let their child "come out to play."

There are also several activities in this section of *Warm Ups & Wind Downs* that are designed to be used at the beginning and the end of the workshop. These activities help the trainer to assess where the participants are in their understanding of the material presented in the workshop and to test the learning climate as well.

Activity 1
# Sign In/Sign Out

**Time:**

5 minutes

**Number of People:**

Unlimited

**Materials/Preparation:**

Newsprint, markers, and tape.

Post the newsprint around the room. Place the markers near the newsprint.

**To Begin:**

- Instruct the participants to "sign in" on the newsprint using the hand they do *not* ordinarily use to write.
- Have them leave a full space between the names.
- Ask the participants how it felt to sign their names with their "other hands." Ask how writing with the "other hand" is like coming into a new situation.
- Leave the newsprint posted or save it for the end of the class or workshop.

**To End:**

- Post the "sign in" newsprint again.
- Ask the participants to sign out using the hand they normally use to write.
- How does writing with your usual hand compare to the end of the workshop or class?
- How do the two experiences compare?

### Activity 2
# A Day of Feelings

**Time:**

5 to 8 minutes for each procedure

**Number of People:**

Unlimited

**Materials/Preparation:**

Music tape and tape player

## Procedure I:

**To Begin:**

- Play the tape. It should be an easy, rhythmic kind of music.
- Instruct the group to move around the room to the rhythm, pantomiming how they are feeling about beginning this new experience. Allow three minutes for this activity.

**To End:**

- Ask the group what feelings they saw pantomimed.
- Ask for volunteers to share what feelings they pantomimed.

## Procedure II:

**To Begin:**

- Halfway through the workshop or class, play the same tape again, instructing the participants to pantomime the feelings they are having now.

**To End:**

- Ask the group if the feelings they saw pantomimed were different from the feelings pantomimed at the beginning of the workshop.
- Ask for volunteers to share their feelings.

# Procedure III:

**To Begin:**

- At the end of the workshop or class, play the tape again.
- Instruct the participants to pantomime the feelings they are having now, at the end of the workshop or class.

**To End:**

- Ask the group what feelings they saw pantomimed, and how those feelings are different from the ones expressed earlier in the workshop or class.
- Ask for volunteers to share their current feelings and how those feelings have changed over the period of the workshop or class.

Activity 3
# Cheers

**Time:**

5 to 8 minutes

**Number of People:**

Unlimited

**Materials/Preparation:**

None

**To Begin:**

- Instruct the participants to form one large circle around the room.

- The group will be doing an old cheer that will help them put names and faces together.

- Give the following example using your own name. Take one step into the circle and call out your name. Tell the group to say, "Mary Jones, she's our woman. If she can't do it...." The person on your left moves one step into the circle and calls out his or her name and says, "John Smith can...." The group says, "John Smith, he's our man. If he can't do it...." The next person to the left steps in and says (using her name), "Susan Brown can...."

- Start a clapping rhythm and begin with your own name as you did in the example.

**To End:**

- Lead the group in a "Yea Team" and applaud.

## Activity 4
# Many Ways to Say Hello

**Time:**

5 to 10 minutes

**Number of People:**

Unlimited

**Materials/Preparation:**

Slips of paper and a bag or basket.

Write the words for "hello" on individual slips of paper. Repeat the words as is necessary for each participant to receive a word. The leader may wish to add words of nationalities represented in the workshop or class.

## Words for Hello

| | | |
|---|---|---|
| 1. O'la | | Italian |
| 2. Heda | | German |
| 3. Buenos dias | | Spanish |
| 4. Neno la kusalimu rafiki au mtani | | Swahili |
| 5. Aloha | | Hawaiian |
| 6. Salut | | French |
| 7. Comment allex-vous | | French |
| 8. Selamat datang | | Malaysian |
| 9. Zdravstvul | | Russian |
| 10. Sayonara | | Japanese |
| 11. Shalom | | Hebrew |
| 12. She you | | Native American (Cherokee) |

**Note:** These words and phrases are forms of greeting, not literal translations of the word "hello."

**To Begin:**

- Ask the participants to form a circle (if there is no room, the participants may stand at their desks).

- Place slips of paper in a basket or bag and have each person draw one.

- The participants will say their words and then say their names in turn around the circle. Tell them to do the best they can with the pronunciations.

**To End:**

- Tell the participants that all nationalities and cultures have words to greet one another.
- Ask for volunteers to name some other things that all nationalities and cultures have in common.

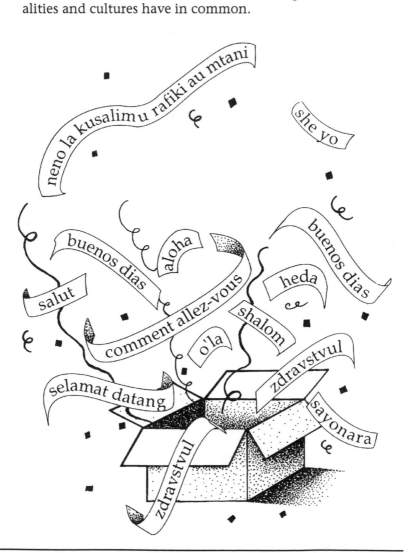

Activity 5

# Birthday Party

**Time:**

10 minutes

**Number of People:**

Unlimited

**Materials/Preparation:**

None

**To Begin:**

- Tell the participants that you will be moving to different parts of the room. Each time you move you will call out a different birthday month.

- The participants will go to where you are standing when their month is called and introduce themselves to the other people in their birthday month. They will also share a memorable birthday with the rest of the group.

- If there is only one person in a month, they should join the month before or after their birthday.

**To End:**

- Ask for volunteers to share the most interesting birthday memory they heard in their group.

Activity 6
# Country Time

**Time:**

10 minutes

**Number of People:**

Unlimited

**Materials/Preparation:**

None

**To Begin:**

- Ask the participants to stand and start a 4-beat clapping rhythm. Prepare yourself as the leader to speak to the rhythm of the clapping as if you were calling a square dance. Tell the participants to follow the instructions they will hear called out.

- Read the following in rhythm:

> *"Find someone you do not know*
> *Shake a hand and say hello."*
> (clap clap clap clap) (clap clap clap clap)
> (Repeat the clapping sequence.)
> *"Now everybody look alive*
> *Give your partner a big high 5."*
> (clap clap clap clap) (clap clap clap clap)
> *"Now you two go and find two more."*
> (clap clap clap clap)
> *"I want to see that group of four."*
> (clap clap clap clap)

*"High 5 around your group of 4*
*Then go on out and find 4 more."*
(clap clap clap clap) (clap clap clap clap)
(Repeat the clapping sequence.)
*"Now each group should be the same*
*Say hello and give your name."*
(clap clap clap clap) (clap clap clap clap)
(Repeat clapping sequence.)

**To End:**

- You may wish to instruct the participants to sit with their new groups for an activity.

Activity 7
# What's Your Recipe?

**Time:**

20 to 25 minutes

**Number of People:**

Unlimited (divided into small groups)

**Materials/Preparation:**

Newsprint and markers

**To Begin:**

- Tell the groups that they will each be writing a recipe for how they are going to work together.

- Explain that the ingredients in the recipe will be the things they believe will help the group work effectively together. Cooperation, enthusiasm, and listening skills are examples of ingredients that could be included in the recipe.

- The groups will write their recipes on newsprint exactly as they would write a recipe for a cake or casserole.

- Ask the groups to post their recipes and share with the other participants.

**To End:**

- Note similarities in the recipes. Ask the participants what they think are the three most important ingredients for working together in a group.

### Activity 8
# Let's Make Friends

**Time:**

10 to 12 minutes

**Number of People:**

Unlimited

**Materials/Preparation:**

Chalkboard or newsprint and markers

**To Begin:**

- Ask the participants to brainstorm things people do to make friends or get acquainted with others. List all the ideas on a board or newsprint.

- Instruct the participants to leave their seats; find someone they do not know and make friends without speaking.

- At the end of one minute, instruct the participants to find someone else they do not know and again try to make friends without speaking.

- At the end of one minute, instruct the participants to find another person they do not know and make friends the regular way.

- At the end of one minute, the participants may find partners one and two and say anything they need to say.

- Look at the brainstorm list and note how many ideas the participants actually used to get acquainted with others.

**To End:**

- Have the participants discuss the difference communicating verbally and non-verbally made in trying to get acquainted.

Activity 9
# Give to Get

**Time:**

10 to 15 minutes

**Number of People:**

Unlimited (divided into small groups)

**Materials/Preparation:**

Index cards, pencils, and rubber bands

**To Begin:**

- Distribute cards and pencils to the groups.
- Instruct the participants to write one thing they want to get from this workshop or class and one thing they can give to the workshop or class on one side of their cards.
- Tell them to write their names on the other side of their cards.
- Ask the participants to share with their groups what they wrote.
- Place the index cards, name side up, in a pile.
- Put a rubber band around each pile and set them aside.

**To End:**

- At the end of the class or workshop, pass the cards back to the participants.
- Instruct the participants to share in their group whether they got what they wanted from the training experience and what they felt they gave to the learning process.

## Activity 10
# 'Round the World

**Time:**

10 to 15 minutes

**Number of People:**

Unlimited

**Materials/Preparation:**

Large map of the world, country, or state. The map should be chosen according to the general make-up of the group. Map pins or colored thumbtacks.

Post the map.

**To Begin:**

- Give all participants a map pin.
- Instruct the participants to place their pins on the map to show where they are from.
- Invite the participants who are from more distant places to share differences and similarities.
- Ask the other participants to share one interesting fact about their hometowns or birthplaces.

**To End:**

- Ask for volunteers to share what is personally special about the places they identified on the map.

Activity 11
# Did You Know?

**Time:**

10 to 15 minutes

**Number of People:**

4 to 30

**Materials/Preparation:**

Prior to the workshop, ask each group member to provide some personal information that he or she is willing to share. You should ask for two or three facts that are unique to that person. Encourage them to brag a little. List one fact about each participant on a sheet of paper and make enough copies for everyone in the workshop or class. For example your list might say:

1. Loves hiking in the wilderness

2. Has won prizes for swimming

3  Is one of a family of 10 children

**To Begin:**

- Distribute the lists to the participants.

- Instruct the participants to find the people who match the statements on the list. The name of the appropriate person should be written next to the matching statement.

**To End:**

- Ask for volunteers to share some of the things they learned about the group.

## Activity 12
# Ape Over Alice

**Time:**

10 to 15 minutes

**Number of People:**

10 to 30

**Materials/Preparation:**

Nametags, basket, or bag.

Prepare the name tags ahead of time for all participants. Write the first name in large letters, and the last name much smaller.

**To Begin:**

- Ask the participants to form a circle. Place a basket of nametags in the center of the circle.

- Tell the participants that they will be taking turns drawing nametags from the basket.

- Explain that they are to come up with a word that describes a feeling and starts with the same letter as the name they draw. They are then to make a statement about the person including their feeling word and the person's name. For example, if the name "Ed" is drawn, one could say, "I am excited about Ed."

- After making the statement, the participants should give the nametag to the owner and shake that person's hand and say hello.

- Continue this activity until everyone has given and received a nametag.

**To End:**

- Tell the participants you are either:
    - a. crazy about the class
    - b. wild about the workshop
    - c. ga ga over the group
    - d. begging to begin

Activity 13
# Collections

**Time:**

12 minutes

**Number of People:**

Unlimited

**Materials/Preparation:**

Copies of collections list below as handouts.

**Collect the names of:**

1  person with an unusual shoe size _____

2  left handed people _____

3  people with the same name as a relative of yours _____

4  people with out of state birthplaces _____

5  people who are dog owners _____

6  people who can sing(they have to sing for you)_____

7  people with brown eyes_____

8  middle names of people (write them down) _____

   _____

9  people wearing white _____

   _____

10  people who say they are happy _____

    _____

**To Begin:**

- Distribute copies of collections list to the participants.
- Tell the participants that they are to write the names of the people they collect on the sheet.
- If the group is large (over 60 people), they can only use a name once.
- Allow 10 minutes for the activity.

**To End:**

- Ask how many participants collected all 55 names.
- Ask for volunteers to share some of the information they collected.

Activity 14
# Get on the Bus

**Time:**

15 minutes

**Number of People:**

4 to 30

**Materials/Preparation:**

Index cards, pencils

**To Begin:**

- Distribute an index card to each participant.
- Tell the participants that you are beginning a journey together. Tell them to think of the room as a huge bus and of you as the driver.
- Explain that the index cards are their tickets.
- Instruct the participants to write their names on one side of their "tickets" and what they hope to get from the day on the other. Assure the participants that no one will read these without their permission.
- Collect the tickets.
- Ask for volunteers to share what they wrote.

**To End:**

- At the end of the workshop, pass the "ticket" back to the participants.
- Ask them how the trip was for them.

Activity 15
# Two and Counting

**Time:**

15 minutes

**Number of People:**

Unlimited (divided into small groups)

**Materials/Preparation:**

None

**To Begin:**

- Instruct the group members to count the number of anatomical feet they have in their families (four for a dog, two for a child, and so forth) and to share with the rest of their group a little bit about those feet (who they belong to, and so forth).

- Total the number of feet represented in the groups at the end of the sharing.

- Ask for the totals, and recognize the group with the largest total.

**To End:**

- Ask for volunteers to share interesting information they learned about other group members.

## Activity 16
# The Basket of Gifts

**Time:**

15 minutes

**Number of People:**

4 to 30

**Materials/Preparation:**

Basket or box, gift wrapped box for each participant

**To Begin:**

- Distribute the gift boxes to the participants with instructions not to open them.

- Place the basket or box at the front of the room where all can see it.

- Explain to the group that everyone has special gifts which will help the whole group to work more effectively together. Use yourself as an example. You might say, "I have brought the gift of enthusiasm to this group, because I am excited about working with all of you."

- Instruct the group to bring their gifts to the front of the room, one at a time, and explain what the gifts are and place them in the basket.

**Note:** You may pass the basket around and have the participants stand where they are.

**To End:**

- Ask the participants if anyone in the group had difficulty thinking of a gift.

- Ask if we need a mixture of gifts to make a group work more effectively.

## Activity 17
# Introducing....

**Time:**

15 minutes

**Number of People:**

4 to 30

**Materials/Preparation:**

Index cards, one per participant

**To Begin:**

- Distribute the index cards and ask the participants to write their names and something they have accomplished that gives them a feeling of pride.
- Collect the cards.
- Tell the participants to stand up when they are introduced.
- Read the name on the index card by saying, "Introducing the great" or "the wonderful" and saying the name.
- Continue by reading what the person accomplished.
- Lead applause for each person.
- Note; you may have the participants draw a card and introduce each other.

**To End:**

- Tell the participants how exciting it is to be working with a group which has already accomplished such great things.

Activity 18
# Data Bank

**Time:**

15 to 20 minutes

**Number of People:**

Unlimited (divided into small groups)

**Materials/Preparation:**

None

**To Begin:**

- Tell the participants that their wallets are like the files in their personal data banks.

- The participants are to pull something from their wallets that accesses particular information about themselves.

- Have that information shared in small groups. As an example, you may hold up your credit card and tell the group about why you need a credit card in your job or about something interesting that you charged.

**To End:**

- Ask the groups to share interesting information they learned about other group members.

## Activity 19
# Tucked Away

**Time:**

15 to 20 minutes

**Number of People:**

Unlimited (divided into small groups)

**Materials/Preparation:**

None

**To Begin:**

- Instruct the participants to think about the places in their homes where things are tucked away. It could be an attic, basement, garage, shed, or storage closet.
- Tell the participants to mentally rummage around in that place and find something that has some special meaning.
- Ask the participants to share their "special something" with their small group.

**To End:**

- Ask the small groups if there was anything particularly unusual that someone shared.
- Ask the participants for interesting things they learned about other group members during this activity.

Activity 20
# Something in Common

**Time:**

15 to 20 minutes

**Number of People:**

Unlimited

**Materials/Preparation:**

None

**To Begin:**

- Tell the participants to pair up with someone they do not know.

- Instruct the participants to find one thing they have in common with their partners outside of this training.

- Allow two minutes for the partners to talk.

- At the end of two minutes, ask for volunteers to share with the group what they found in common with their partner.

- Tell the participants to find someone else they do not know.

- Instruct the participants to find two things they have in common with their partner outside of this training.

- Allow four minutes for partners to talk.

- At the end of four minutes ask for volunteers to share the two things they found in common with their partner, with the whole group.

- If this is a large group, find one more partner to share three things they have in common and then share with the large group.

**To End:**

- Ask the participants what they found to be the most frequent categories they had in common; example: family, food, and so forth.

Activity 21
# Categories

**Time:**

15 to 25 minutes

**Number of People:**

6 to 40

**Materials/Preparation:**

None

**To Begin:**

1. Have the participants form a circle sitting down.

2. Begin a four beat clapping rhythm by slapping left hand on left thigh (clap #1) right hand on right thigh (clap #2) and hands together twice (clap #3) (clap #4). The entire circle should be clapping the rhythm.

3. Begin by calling out the first category, "names" and then during the next four beats call out your own name. The person on your left will call out his name on the next four beats and so on all the way around the circle.

4. When it comes around to you, call out a new category and continue around the circle.

5. You may choose as many or as few categories as you have time for.

6. You may allow the group to come up with their own categories.

## Suggested Subjects

Names (always first)

| | |
|---|---|
| Favorite place | Favorite foods |
| Best vacation | Birthplace |
| Favorite TV show | Love to do |
| Right now I feel.. | Really want... |
| Don't like | Favorite song |

**To End:**

- Ask the participants to share something they learned about someone in the circle.

## Activity 22
# Pairs

**Time:**

15 minutes

**Number of People:**

6 to 40

**Materials/Preparation:**

Small slips of paper with one word from the pair list written on each slip. Be sure to use only as many words as there are people. Every word must have its mate included as well.

**To Begin:**

- Place all paper slips in a box and mix. Pass the box so each participant can draw. If the group number is uneven, include the leader.

- Tell the participants that each word is one half of a pair. They have two minutes to find their other half.

- Instruct the participants to introduce themselves to their partners and to share why they are here. They have three minutes to do so.

- Now instruct the pairs to find another pair to make a foursome, introduce themselves, and share one hobby. They have three minutes.

- You may continue this process to groups of 8, 16 and so forth until you have one big group.

## Pairs

| | |
|---|---|
| salt | pepper |
| granny | grandpa |
| mom | pop |
| spaghetti | meat balls |
| shoes | socks |
| sugar | cream |
| bread | butter |
| thunder | lightening |
| boy | girl |
| cats | dogs |
| heart | soul |
| table | chairs |
| birds | bees |
| heaven | earth |
| peanut butter | jelly |
| comb | brush |
| bacon | eggs |
| knife | fork |
| you | me |
| aunt | uncle |

**To End:**
- Ask the participants for something interesting they learned about another group member.

Activity 23
# What's on Your Mind?

**Time:**

20 minutes

**Number of People:**

4 to 30

**Materials/Preparation:**

Newsprint and markers.

Post blank newsprint around the room. Place the markers nearby.

**To Begin:**

- After welcoming the participants and reviewing the agenda, explain that most people come to a new experience such as this training or class with questions and concerns.

- Instruct the participants to write one question, concern or interest they may have on the newsprint provided.

- After all the participants have had an opportunity to write, read each question or statement aloud.

- If a question will be addressed during the training/class, write the appropriate time (and day) when it will be covered, on the newsprint next to the question.

- If a question/concern will not be addressed during the training/class, suggest resources, or offer to identify resources after the training/class has ended.

- Be sure to address anything that is written on the newsprint.

- Ask if there are any additions to the list before moving on.

- Keep the list posted during the training/class.

**To End:**

- When the training/class is over, review the questions and concerns to ensure that they were addressed.

Activity 24
# Slogans

**Time:**

20 minutes

**Number of People:**

Unlimited (divided into small groups)

**Materials/Preparation:**

Newsprint, markers

**To Begin:**

- Instruct each participant to think of a popular slogan that describes him or her.
- Give an example. You might say, "Have it your way" is your slogan because, as the trainer or leader, you want to meet the needs of the group.
- Have the participants share their slogans with their small groups and explain why they chose a particular slogan.
- Ask them to brainstorm some slogans that could describe the workshop or class.
- Record all of the ideas on newsprint and post.

**To End:**

- At the conclusion of the workshop, ask for a vote on the best slogan to describe the workshop.

## Activity 25
# Bouncing for Names

**Time:**

20 minutes

**Number of People:**

6 to 30

**Materials/Preparation:**

Ball for bouncing

**To Begin:**

- The participants will form a circle and hand one person the ball.

- The person with the ball will start it bouncing, saying the first letter of his or her first name and then his or her name and then a sentence that uses the first letter of the name. For example, "A. My name is Alan and I eat apples." "L. My name is Linda and I like lizards."

- As soon as the first person completes his or her sentence, he or she bounces the ball to the person on his or her left. The bouncing rhythm is maintained until the ball has been all the way around the circle.

**To End:**

- Mention the name of a participant and see who can remember what that person said. Do that several times, choosing a variety of people.

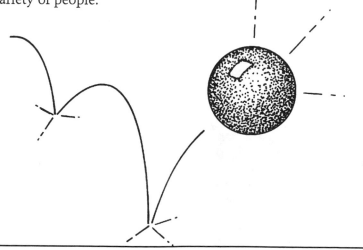

Activity 26
# Personalized License Plates

**Time:**

20 minutes

**Number of People:**

Unlimited (divided into small groups)

**Materials/Preparation:**

8 ¹/₂ x 11 card board folded length-wise, one piece per participant, markers.

**To Begin:**

- Distribute cardboard and pens.
- Tell the participants that they will be making personalized
  license plates.
- Ask them to think of a word or letters and numbers that have
  personal meaning and put them on the cardboard. The result
  should resemble a license plate from their state.
- Have the participants put their license plates in front of them
  tent style on the tables, so that other group members can read
  them.
- Share the meaning of the license plates with other group
  members.

**To End:**

- Ask for volunteers to share some of the most unique plate
  with the other groups.

Activity 27

# Fact and Fiction

**Time:**

20 minutes

**Number of People:**

Unlimited (divided into small groups)

**Materials/Preparation:**

None

**To Begin:**

- Instruct the group members to take turns sharing two facts and one fiction about themselves. The rest of the group is to guess what is and is not true.

- Start by sharing two facts and one fiction about yourself and asking the participants to guess what is and is not true.

**To End:**

- Ask the participants what interesting facts they learned about others.

- Ask the question, "How is fact sometimes stranger than fiction?"

Activity 28
# Odds and Ends

**Time:**

20 to 25 minutes

**Number of People:**

4 to 30 (divided into small groups)

**Materials/Preparation:**

Basket or bucket, variety of small objects from the house, the outdoors, the office or the classroom. For example: a spool of thread, small toys, leaves or flowers, paper clips, chalk.

**To Begin:**

- Pass the basket and instruct the participants to choose one object from it.
- Explain to the participants that they chose a particular object because of some association they have with it.
- Each participant is to share in small groups the meaning the object has for him or her. For example: "I chose the spool of thread because I sew or because I feel wound up tight."

**To End:**

- Ask for volunteers to talk about some of the interesting things that were shared in their groups.

## Activity 29
# Autograph Frisbees

**Time:**

25 minutes

**Number of People:**

Unlimited

**Materials/Preparation:**

Paper plates and pencils

**To Begin:**

- Distribute paper plates and pencils.
- Instruct the participants to write their names on their paper plates.
- Place an object as a marker on the floor in an open area of the room, or outside.
- Tell the participants to bring their plates and pencils, stand, and make a circle around the object.
- The participants will throw their paper plate toward the object on the count of three.
- They will then pick up someone else's paper plate and return to their places in the circle.
- The participants will autograph the plate they now have and toss the plate at the object again, at the count of three.
- Repeat the process, with the participants choosing another plate and autographing it.
- The third time, the participants should find their own plates again.
- Instruct the participants to find the two people who have autographed their plates and share two things about themselves.

**To End:**

- Ask for volunteers to share something interesting they learned about another member of the workshop/class.

## Activity 30
# Hangups

**Time:**

25 minutes

**Number of People:**

4 to 30

**Materials/Preparation:**

Wire coat hangers, cardboard, crayons and markers, scissors, decorative materials, string, clothes line.

String the clothes line across a corner of the room.

**To Begin:**

- Distribute the materials including one wire coat hanger to each participant.
- Tell the participants to make a mobile that tells some things about themselves. Their names must be hanging from somewhere on the mobile.
- Hang the mobiles from the line following completion.

**To End:**

- Ask the participants to talk about their mobiles to the rest of the group.

Activity 31

# Picture Matching

**Time:**

30 minutes

**Number of People:**

4 to 30

**Materials/Preparation:**

Plain paper, markers, crayons

**To Begin:**

- Tell the participants to work alone and draw a self portrait. Ask them not to share their portraits with anyone else.

- After all have completed their portraits, collect them and hang them up across the front of the room.

- Beginning at the right side of the room, instruct one participant at a time to match someone with his or her portrait. The participant should do this by choosing someone and placing the person beneath his or her portrait. If the match is correct, the person whose portrait it is should sign his name at the bottom of the portrait and sit down.

- If the match is not correct, both people should return to their seats.

- The game continues until all portraits are signed.

**To End:**

- Allow the participants to take the portraits home at the end of the workshop.

## Activity 32
# You Deserve a Medal

**Time:**

45 minutes

**Number of People:**

4 to 30

**Materials/Preparation:**

Cardboard (preferably in colors), string or ribbon, glitter, tinsel, stars, foil or other decorative materials, scissors

Cut 3" circles out of cardboard. Punch a hole in the cardboard near an edge. Cut ribbon or string into 16" to 20" lengths.

**To Begin:**

- Instruct the participants to print their first names in the center of their medals.

- Ask the participants to think of an accomplishment of which they are especially proud, (winning a race, cooking a meal, writing a poem).

- Instruct the participants to decorate their medals as if they had received them for the accomplishment.

- When the participants have completed their medals, ask them to thread them with the ribbons and tie them around their necks.

- Encourage the participants to share their accomplishments with the group.

**To End:**

- Ask the participants why it is important to recognize what you do well and reward yourself.

Activity 33
# Hats Off to You

**Time:**

45 minutes

**Number of People:**

4 to 30

**Materials/Preparation:**

Paper painters hats (available in most paint stores), ribbon, stars, stickers, flowers, feathers, magic markers, plain white paper, stapler, tape scissors.

Staple strips of plain paper over the words on the hats.

**To Begin:**

- Distribute hats and instruct the participants to print their first names or the name they like to be called on the front of their hats.

- Spread out decorative materials, tape, and staplers in a central place and invite the group to decorate their hats with these materials.

- Encourage the participants to design their hats in ways that are uniquely their own and that reveal some things about themselves.

**To End:**

- Invite the participants to explain their hat designs with other group members.

## Training Notes

Records of the activities used with various groups and the effectiveness of those activities are useful tools for the group leader or trainer in planning future workshops.

| Activity | Date/Group | Notes |
|---|---|---|
| _____ | _____ | _____ |
| _____ | _____ | _____ |
| _____ | _____ | _____ |
| _____ | _____ | _____ |
| _____ | _____ | _____ |
| _____ | _____ | _____ |
| _____ | _____ | _____ |
| _____ | _____ | _____ |
| _____ | _____ | _____ |
| _____ | _____ | _____ |
| _____ | _____ | _____ |
| _____ | _____ | _____ |
| _____ | _____ | _____ |
| _____ | _____ | _____ |
| _____ | _____ | _____ |

# Chapter II
# Group Building

# Introduction

Groups have a pattern they follow as they move toward working together productively. Often, the time constraints of a training or workshop do not allow the group to spontaneously follow this pattern. Group building activities can, however, artificially accelerate the process.

When groups form, they are simply clusters of individuals experiencing various levels of anxiety at the prospect of interacting with others in a strange setting. The leader or trainer can reduce this anxiety gradually, by choosing activities initially that involve low personal risk. These are activities that require the participants to interact but do not require personal revelations or "sharing." Later, activities requiring increased levels of personal risk can safely be introduced.

Group work is an effective approach to the learning process. It allows for more thorough processing of information and provides a structure for the exchange of ideas. Often, grouping the participants reduces the fear of speaking out or asking questions that individuals may bring to a larger group.

Grouping is also a means of managing a large number of people. Experiential activities and skill practice, for example, work best in small groups, as do processing and cooperative learning. Indeed, if a goal of the workshop or training is for the participants to interact with the material in any way, then grouping is a necessity.

In order to build effective groups, it is necessary to first dissolve groups who come to the training together. It is easier for the participants to cling to old ideas and behaviors when there is support from friends or colleagues. Subgroups also interfere with the group process, sabotaging group efforts to become a working unit.

There are occasions when a leader may wish to regroup the participants to accomplish a particular learning activity. It is important to remember that anytime the makeup of a group changes, a group-building activity will be needed to accommodate that change.

## Activity 34
# Brag Bags

**Time:**

2 to 3 minutes

**Number of People:**

4 to 50

**Materials/Preparation:**

Small brown paper bags (one per participant), markers, thumbtacks.

**To Begin:**

- Distribute bags and thumbtacks to each participant.
- Instruct the participants to write their names in large letters on their bags.
- The participants will tack their bags to the wall in a designated area of the room in a way that leaves the bag open and allows the name to be seen.
- The participants can send positive messages to one another by putting them in the bags.
- Messages may be read at anytime during the workshop, but the bags should not be removed from the wall.

**To End:**

- Have brief message-writing opportunities throughout the workshop.
- Write each participant a message at sometime during the workshop to ensure that all the participants receive a message.
- Bags can be taken home at the end of the workshop.

Activity 35

# You're the Greatest

**Time:**

5 to 10 minutes

**Number of People:**

Unlimited

**Materials/Preparation:**

None

**To Begin:**

- Instruct the participants to form a straight line across the room.

- The participants will be counting off, but instead of numbers they will repeat the words: GREAT, GORGEOUS, TALENTED, BRILLIANT, TERRIFIC, WONDERFUL (use as many words as the number of groups you wish to form).

- Start the counting off, with the first person in line by saying you're great, you're gorgeous, and so forth until the group catches on (you may want to write the words on a poster and hold them up so people can remember the order).

**To End:**

- Tell all the gorgeous people to sit together, all the brilliant people to sit together, and so forth.

Activity 36

# The Paper Chase

**Time:**

10 to 12 minutes

**Number of Participants:**

Unlimited (divided into small groups)

**Materials/Preparation:**

Small stack of plain white paper for each group.

**To Begin:**

- Instruct the participants to brainstorm with their groups as many uses for one piece of plain white paper as possible. The paper cannot be written or drawn on in any way, it must remain blank.

- Tell groups to choose someone to record their ideas.

- Allow four to five minutes for the brainstorming.

- Have the groups choose their best or most original idea to demonstrate to the other groups.

- Allow two to three minutes for groups to make their decision and prepare.

- Ask for a volunteer group to begin the demonstrations.

- Applaud all efforts.

**To End:**

- Have the groups display all of their ideas for the other groups to see.

- Ask the group members what they learned about the way their small group worked together.

Activity 37
# Pick Up a Friend

**Time:**

10 to 15 minutes

**Number of People:**

6 to 50 (teams)

**Materials/Preparation:**

A large open area like a gymnasium or playing field.

Bright colored pillows, beanbags, cones, or other markers.

The markers are used to designate stations. Put the markers out around the edge of the open area. Designate as many stations as there are members on each team. For example, if there are teams of five, there should be five stations marked, including the starting station.

**To Begin:**

- Gather the teams at the starting station. Tell them they will leave one team member at the start and send other team members to each of the other stations to wait.

- At the word "go," the starting team member is to run to a station and pick up the waiting team member. Those two team members must join hands and go to another station to pick up another team member. The team continues until all team members have been picked up and are holding hands. The team should then return to the starting station. The first team in wins.

- Except for the starter, no team member can leave his or her station until he or she has joined hands with another member of the team.

- Teams may pick up their members in any order they wish.

- If competing teams touch each other at all, both teams must return to their stations and begin over again.

- If any team members fall down or drop their hands, that team must return to their stations and begin again.

**To End:**

- When all teams have arrived "home," applaud the winners and the efforts of all.

- Ask the participants what kind of teamwork was involved in playing this game.

## Activity 38
# House of Cards

**Time:**

12 to 15 minutes

**Number of People:**

Unlimited (divided into small groups)

**Materials/Preparation:**

Deck of cards for each small group. You may use half a deck to reduce the difficulty of this activity.

**To Begin:**

- Tell the groups to distribute an even number of cards to each group member. Discard the leftover cards.

- The groups have seven minutes to build a house of cards using all the cards the group has. Each group member must place his or her own cards. The group should decide in what order they should be placed and can offer suggestions and encouragement to each other.

- Tell groups to start when you call "go" and end when you call "stop."

**To End:**

- Ask the groups what difficulties they encountered during this activity.

- Ask group members what they learned about the way their group worked together.

- Ask the groups if it would be easier to do this task a second time.

**Note:** Time permitting you can have them do the activity again following the same procedure.

## Activity 39
# Fascinatin' Feud

**Time:**

15 minutes

**Number of People:**

Unlimited (divided into small groups)

**Materials/Preparation:**

Copies of the following story. Each story should be cut into strips, one sentence per strip.

**To Begin:**

- Give a complete set of story strips to each small group. Make sure the order of the strips is mixed up.
- Groups should divide the strips equally among group members.
- The task is to put the strips in an order that forms a story with a beginning, a middle, and an end.
- They are not to start until the leader says go.
- Explain that each group member must place his or her own strips in the story. Other group members may contribute suggestions and advice. The story must make sense all the way through.
- Set a time limit.
- Say "go."

**To End:**

- Ask the groups what they learned about working together during this exercise.

**Note:** Some groups will finish well ahead of others. All groups should be allowed to finish.


- The Trembles and the Prickles were always feuding.
- Some say it started when Elias Tremble went away to join the army.
- He left Lizzy Prickle at the alter.

- Others say it started when Sheriff Dan Tremble arrested Pete Prickle for fighting.
- Pete had a heart attack in jail and died.
- Now trouble was brewing again between the Trembles and the Prickles.
- It seems that Ellie Mae Tremble was out walking in the woods.
- She was looking for a Jack-in-the Pulpit.
- This is a kind of plant that looks like a preacher standing in the pulpit of a church.
- Ellie Mae liked to dig them up and take them home and plant them in her garden.
- Josh Prickle was also walking in the woods that day.
- He was carrying his axe.
- He chopped down a small tree.
- Ellie Mae was nearby and heard it fall.
- Seconds later she felt a sting on her arm.
- The arm was bleeding.
- She ran home holding her injured arm.
- The Trembles called the Sheriff.
- The Sheriff arrested Josh.
- He told the Sheriff he had chopped down a tree and nothing more.
- They found the fallen tree where Josh said it would be.
- There was a piece of bark from the fallen tree near where Ellie Mae had been standing.
- The Sheriff let Josh go.
- Josh sent Ellie Mae flowers.
- Ellie Mae loved the flowers and invited him to supper.
- The feud may be coming to an end with this courting couple.

Activity 40

# Live and Learn

**Time:**

15 to 20 minutes

**Number of People:**

Unlimited (divided into small groups)

**Materials/Preparation:**

None

**To Begin:**

- Ask the participants to partner with someone in their group.

- Instruct each partner to think of something about his or her heritage, culture or ethnic group that is unique and interesting and teach it to the other partner. It could be a song, a saying, a ritual or tradition or just a bit of history or information.

- After both partners have had the opportunity to teach each other, they will take turns teaching the group what they learned about their partner's heritage.

**To End:**

- Ask the participants what similarities they noted in the different backgrounds of group members.

Activity 41
# Erector Set

**Time:**

15 to 25 minutes

**Number of People:**

4 to 50 (divided into small groups)

**Materials/Preparation:**

Small slips of paper with names of buildings written on them.

| | |
|---|---|
| school | fire station |
| apartment house | bank |
| restaurant | department store |
| barn | parking garage |
| church/synagogue | |

**To Begin:**

- Distribute slips of paper, one per group and instruct the participants to keep their assignments secret from the other groups.
- Tell the participants they are to use the bodies of all group members to build their buildings. Tell the groups they may make noises and use movement, but they cannot speak. Allow five to six minutes for the groups to work.
- Ask each group to "perform" and other groups to guess what building the performers have built.
- Applaud all efforts.

**To End:**

- Ask the participants what they learned about working together in a group.

Activity 42
# An Olympic Event

**Time:**

15 to 30 minutes

**Number of People:**

6 to 30

**Materials/Preparation:**

Batons, one for each team (can be rolled newspaper, paper towel rolls or sticks). A walking course marked off at even intervals (the number of intervals should equal the number of members of each team) with a starting and finish line. For example: If two teams of 10 are competing, you could mark a one mile walking course at 1/10 mile intervals.

**To Begin:**

- Tell the participants that they will be part of the newest Olympic Event, walking backwards.
- Explain that one member of each team will start, carrying a baton, and walk backwards to the first interval marker. At that point another team member will be waiting to take the baton and continue to the next marker.
- Each team member should have an opportunity to race. (If there are not enough team members to complete the course, a team member may race twice.)
- Give the teams a few minutes to develop their strategy.
- Line starting members up at the starting line and say "Go."
- Congratulate the winners.

**To End:**

- Ask the participants how they felt about the competition.
- Ask them what kind of teamwork was necessary to run this race.

## Activity 43
# Painter's Palette

**Time:**

20 minutes

**Number of People:**

6 to 50

**Materials/Preparation:**

None

**To Begin:**

- Instruct the participants to line up and count off by colors: RED, GREEN, BLUE, YELLOW, ORANGE, PURPLE. Use as many colors as needed to form groups of six to eight.

- Instruct the participants to work with their color groups to come up with a thirty second presentation around their color. For example: the groups could think of things that are that color or feelings the color represents.

- Allow 5 to 10 minutes for the groups to work on their presentations.

- Have each color group do their presentation before the rest of the participants.

- Applaud all efforts.

**To End:**

- Ask the group members what they had to do to work together to come up with a presentation.

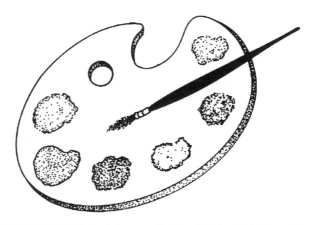

Sandra Peyser Hazouri and Miriam Smith McLaughlin

Activity 44
# What If....

**Time:**

20 minutes

**Number of People:**

Unlimited (divided into small groups)

**Materials/Preparation:**

Small slips of paper with "What if" statements written on them, newsprint, magic markers

**To Begin:**

* Distribute one slip of paper to each group.

* Instruct each group to assign a recorder.

* Tell the groups to brainstorm and record ideas around the "what if" statements on the newsprint. Allow 8 to 10 minutes for brainstorming.

* Invite each group to share their "what if" statements and the ideas they recorded with the other groups.

* Applaud all efforts.

## What If:

* money grew on trees

* dogs could get drivers licenses

* the President of the US was a 10-year-old girl

* wearing shoes was illegal

* you had to be 30 years old to eat pizza

* all people looked exactly alike

* chocolate grew everywhere like wildflowers

* there were no traffic lights

**To End:**

* Before your presentation, answer these questions in your small group:

    a. Did everyone in your group participate?

    b. Did different people play different roles in your group?

    c. Were all ideas written down or did your group screen ideas?

Activity 45

# Shopping Spree

**Time:**

20 minutes

**Number of People:**

Unlimited (divided into small groups)

**Materials/Preparation:**

None

**To Begin:**

- Announce to the participants that they each have $500 to spend. Tell them the money is special because it can only buy intangibles like health, love, adventure, beauty, wisdom, and so forth.

- Instruct the participants to share with their small group how they would spend the money. Allow three minutes per person sharing time.

- Each group may want to list their qualities on newsprint.

**To End:**

- Ask the participants if there were any unusual answers.

- Ask the participants what they learned about another group member or themselves.

Activity 46
# Locomotion

**Time:**

20 minutes

**Number of People:**

6 to 30 (divided into small groups)

**Materials/Preparation:**

Small slips of paper.

Write the names of the various forms of transportation on individuals slips of paper. TRUCK, TRAIN, BUS, AIRPLANE, MO-TORCYCLE, SUBWAY, SHIP, SAILBOAT, GOLF CART, FIRE EN-GINE, CAR, BICYCLE.

**To Begin:**

- Allow the groups to draw a slip of paper.
- Tell the groups their task will be to form a sculpture in motion, using all group members, that portrays whatever mode of transportation they drew.
- The groups should keep their assignment secret from other groups.
- After the groups have had an opportunity to design their living sculpture, ask them to present to the rest of the class.
- Other participants should guess what the different sculptures portray.
- Applaud all efforts.

**To End:**

- Have each group tell the others two ways society benefits from this mode of transportation.
- Ask each group what they learned about the way their group worked together.

Activity 47
# Footprints

**Time:**

20 minutes

**Number of People:**

4 to 30

**Materials/Preparation:**

Plain white paper, felt tip pens, markers, or pencils.

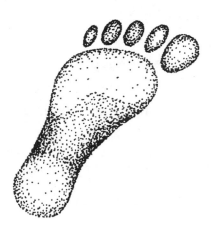

**To Begin:**

- Ask the participants to form a circle.

- Distribute paper and pens.

- Instruct the participants to place the paper on the floor and trace around his or her right foot, (with or without shoes).

- Leave the paper in place and step one position to the left.

- Instruct the participants to "try on" the footprint in front of them.

- Does it fit?

- Leave the paper in place and step one more place to the left.

- Try on this footprint.

**To End:**

- Ask the participants why their foot does not fit anyone else's footprint.

- Ask them what they would have to do to make a "fit."

- Ask what other ways people are "different."

Activity 48

# Group Portrait

**Time:**

20 to 25 minutes

**Number of People:**

Unlimited (divided into small groups)

**Materials/Preparation:**

Newsprint, markers, masking tape.

**To Begin:**

- Tell the groups they are to draw a composite group picture. In other words, the group should draw one figure that is representative of the whole group. For example, if one person in the group is a runner, the figure may have on running shoes.

- All group members should participate and should be represented.

**To End:**

- Ask each group to present their portrait to the rest of the participants and to explain how the portrait is representative of their group.

- Applaud all efforts.

Activity 49
# Throw and Go

**Time:**

20 to 25 minutes

**Number of People:**

Unlimited

**Materials/Preparation:**

String or tape to mark start and finish. Pencils, balls of crumpled paper or other objects that will not roll easily. Large open area.

Mark off a starting line and designate a finish line a good distance away. If you are in a gym, a good distance would be from one wall to the opposite wall.

**To Begin:**

- Divide the participants into equal teams of five or six, and instruct the teams to line up one behind the other at the starting line.
- Give the first member of each team an object. (If your game area is small use crumpled paper balls or other objects that cannot be thrown far.)
- Give the teams the following instructions:

## Instructions

1. On go the first team member throws the object and the whole team moves in line to where the object landed.
2. The first team member goes to the back of the line, and the next team member picks up the object and throws it.
3. Again the whole team moves in line to where the object landed. Team member 2 goes to the back of the line and team member 3 picks up the object and throws it.
4. The first team to reach the finish line wins.

5. The object and the first (front) team member must be over the finish line for a win to be called.

6. When the team moves to the object they must stay in line behind the object.

7 If the team gets out of line or moves in front of the object, they must move back to the starting line and begin again.

8. The leading team member is responsible for keeping the team behind the object. Practice to be sure everyone understands how to play.

**To End:**

• Applaud the winners.

• Ask the participants what kinds of teamwork were necessary to play this game.

Activity 50

# The Cart Before the Horse

**Time:**

20 to 30 minutes

**Number of People:**

Unlimited (groups of six or less)

**Materials/Preparation:**

One blindfold for each group, plain paper, pencils.

**To Begin:**

- Tell the participants that they will be working with their groups to draw a picture.

- Explain that each group member will contribute to the drawing according to instructions. The person whose turn it is to draw will be blindfolded. The rest of the group will watch and advise, but may not otherwise assist the person drawing.

- Choose a volunteer to begin and blindfold him or her.

- Distribute one piece of paper and a pencil to each blindfolded participant.

- Read Instruction 1 and allow just 30 seconds for the participants to draw.

- Ask the participants to remove their blindfolds and pass them and the paper to the group members who will be the next to draw.

- As soon as all blindfolds are in place, read Instruction 2. This time, allow more time for the participants to draw.

- Continue passing the blindfold and the drawing until all instructions are completed and all group members have had an opportunity to draw. As the instructions become more detailed, allow more time for the participants to draw.

- Ask groups to post their finished products on the wall and applaud all efforts.

**To End:**

- Ask the participants what helped or hindered their drawing efforts.

# Instructions

1. On the right side of your paper, draw a hill
2. Draw a barn on the hill.
3. To the left of the hill draw a horse.
4. To the left of the horse draw a cart or wagon being pulled by the horse.
5. Draw a man sitting in the cart, holding the horse's reins.
6. Draw a hat and a beard on the man.

Activity 51
# The Auction

**Time:**

25 minutes

**Number of People:**

6 to 50 (divided into small groups)

**Materials/Preparation:**

Large index cards, markers.

Fold the index cards in half to make tents that will stand on their own. Write the words from the following list on individual tent cards in large letters.

HEALTH

PEACE

BEAUTY

JOY

PHYSICAL STRENGTH

TALENT

WEALTH

WISDOM

YOUTH

FAME

COURAGE

POWER

CONTENTMENT

LOVE

**To Begin:**

- Arrange the tent cards so they can be viewed by all the participants.
- Tell the groups that they have fifty dollars to use to bid on any of the items on the table.
- The groups should decide together what they will bid on and how high they will bid.
- The groups will want to have a number of choices as they may not get the first one or two they choose.
- There is only $50 per group. The group members should take turns bidding, and the same group member should bid until the item is sold.
- Once an item is sold, write what it cost on the card and pass it to the purchasing group.
- The leader or a volunteer should serve as the auctioneer.
- The leader will choose an item, hold it up, and ask for bids. Continue until all items are sold.

**To End:**

- Ask the groups why they bid on particular items.
- Talk about how the groups decided on what items they would purchase.

Activity 52
# Buying Happiness

**Time:**

25 minutes

**Number of People:**

4 to 30 (divided into small groups)

**Materials/Preparation:**

Large index cards, markers, paper and pencils.

Fold the index cards in half so they "stand" like tents. On each card write an item from the list on the following page and the price. Arrange the cards on a table.

**To Begin:**

- Tell the participants they each have $50 to spend.
- They will come up to the table and "shop" for the items they wish to purchase.
- Tell them to leave the card on the table, as someone else may wish to buy the same item and to just write down what they want to buy and the cost.
- After the shopping trip, the participants will share with their small groups what they bought and why.

**To End:**

- Ask the participants what they learned about themselves through this activity.

**Note:** You can add to or delete from the following:

- Wide screen TV ....................................... $  10
- New bicycle ........................................... $  10
- Education ............................................... $  25
- Trip around world ................................. $  35
- Porsche ................................................. $  30
- Designer wardrobe ............................... $  15
- Fishing gear .......................................... $   5
- Cruise ................................................... $  10
- Toyota .................................................. $  10
- Boat ...................................................... $  10
- Golf clubs ............................................. $   5
- Live to be 100 yrs old ........................... $  50
- Trip to Hawaii ...................................... $  20
- Become famous ..................................... $  40
- Trip in your state .................................. $   5
- Increase IQ ........................................... $  30
- Diamond ring......................................... $  20
- Cabin in the woods ............................... $  25
- Camping trip.......................................... $   5
- Become president .................................. $  40
- Big house............................................... $  30
- Marry your true love ............................ $  40
- Health ................................................... $  50
- Lifetime movie pass .............................. $   5
- Lifetime NY theater tickets .................. $  15

Activity 53
# State Stats

**Time:**

25 to 30 minutes

**Number of People:**

20 to 30 (divided into small groups)

**Materials/Preparation:**

Newsprint, markers, stick on dots or stars.

**To Begin:**

- Distribute newsprint and markers to each small group.
- Give each participant five dots or stars.
- Tell groups to list on newsprint all the characteristics they think are important, special or unique about their state.
- With all groups participating, go over each list, eliminating all duplications by crossing them out, so that each idea appears only once. For example, if lists number one and two both say "great beaches," you would leave it on one list and cross it out on the other.
- After you have worked through all the lists, the participants will vote for the five characteristics they think are most important about their state. They will vote by placing one dot next to each of the five characteristics on the lists they believe are most important.
- After all the participants have voted, add the dots that are next to each item.
- Announce the consensus of the group by pointing out those items that received the most votes.

**To End:**

- Explain to the participants that this was a consensus activity.
- Note that each person had a say in the final conclusions.
- Ask the participants other ways that their groups might use the consensus process.

Activity 54

# Pioneers

**Time:**

25 to 30 minutes

**Number of People:**

Unlimited (divided into small groups)

**Materials/Preparation:**

Newsprint, markers, index cards.

Write the names of the different "lands" on individual index cards.

## Lands

Candyland (everything in it is made of candy)

Magic Kingdom (all the fairytale characters live here)

Never Never Land (no one ever grows up)

Tropical Paradise (everyone has everything they need)

Land of Milk and Honey (everyone has more than they will ever need)

La La Land (nothing is what it seems to be)

**To Begin:**

- Distribute newsprint, markers and one index card to each group. You may give the same "Land" to more than one group or give the same "Land" to every group.

- Tell groups they are to design a very basic government for their Land. Their design should include 4 or 5 laws for governing people and the means for electing a leader.

- Groups have 15 minutes to work and should develop their government as much as possible during that time.

- Tell them to record the laws and other information about the "Land" on newsprint.

- At the end of 15 minutes, ask groups to post their newsprint and explain their government to the rest of the participants.
- Applaud all efforts.

**To End:**

- Ask the groups to share some of their experience working together on this project.
- You may have the total group vote on where they would prefer to live.

**Note:** Consider choosing "Lands" that are appropriate to the age group with which you are working. While an adult would do well with any of the "Lands" listed above, a young person may find the concepts behind "La La Land" or "Land of Milk and Honey" difficult to grasp.

Activity 55
# Share a Story

**Time:**

30 minutes

**Number of People:**

Unlimited (divided into small groups)

**Materials/Preparation:**

None

**To Begin:**

- Tell the participants to think of a story they would like to share with their groups. It can be something funny, interesting or poignant from their lives.
- They should think of the highlights of the story, as they will be given only two minutes to tell it.
- The groups should choose a time keeper who will signal the teller at the $1^1/_2$ minute mark.
- At the end of each story, the group must ask the story teller two questions.

**To End:**

- Ask for volunteers to share some things they learned about group members from the story telling activity.

# Training Notes

Records of the activities used with various groups and the effectiveness of the activities in particular are useful tools for the group leader or trainer in planning future workshops.

| Activity | Date/Group | Notes |
|---|---|---|
| _____ | _____ | _____ |
| _____ | _____ | _____ |
| _____ | _____ | _____ |
| _____ | _____ | _____ |
| _____ | _____ | _____ |
| _____ | _____ | _____ |
| _____ | _____ | _____ |
| _____ | _____ | _____ |
| _____ | _____ | _____ |
| _____ | _____ | _____ |
| _____ | _____ | _____ |
| _____ | _____ | _____ |
| _____ | _____ | _____ |
| _____ | _____ | _____ |

# Chapter III
# Boosters

# Introduction

Boosters or energizers are often misunderstood training tools. Because they are usually enjoyable, they are sometimes seen as frivolous; detractors from the seriousness of the workshop or training. Otherwise competent trainers will leave out the 'fun and games' citing better use of time as the reason. In doing so, these trainers lose an opportunity to recharge and motivate the participants in ways that can increase their levels of achievement.

Learning theorists tell us that all people have limits to the amount of information they can absorb at any given time. For children and youth, this is, of course, particularly true. Games requiring lots of physical activity and preferably, out-of-doors, should be part of any training for young people. Also, free time, away from the structure of the training, should be incorporated into the training agenda.

Adults need breaks as well. The traditional fifteen minutes for coffee and snacks is, of course, necessary. Such breaks do little, however, to change the pace of a training. An alert trainer will regularly read the mood and tempo of the group and infuse short energizers into the day when participation flags or eyes begin to droop.

The energy in a training room can quickly be rearranged through the use of short activities that are physical, fun or mildly challenging. These activities can be rejuvenating for the participants and trainer alike.

## Activity 56
# Oliver Crumpet for Kids

**Time:**

3 minutes

**Number of People**

(unlimited)

**Materials/Preparation:**

None

**To Begin:**

- Tell the children you will be telling them the story of Oliver Crumpet.
- They are to do all the actions that Oliver does.
- Read the story, and act out what Oliver does along with the children.

**To End:**

- Tell the children to applaud themselves for a job well done.

## Oliver and the Beautiful Pony

Oliver Crumpet *got up out of his chair* one morning and *looked out the window* while *shading his eyes with his hands.* He *looked to the left* and he *looked to the right.* Then he *looked straight across the river.* There he saw a beautiful pony eating grass on the riverbank. "Oh," said Oliver, "Oh my!" He *waved at the pony with his left hand;* he *waved at the pony with his right hand.* He even *jumped up and down.* The pony did not stop eating or look up. Oliver *tapped his chin with his finger.* "What will I do?" he wondered. He *sat back down in his chair.* Suddenly he *clapped his hands.* "I know what I'll do!" he said. He *got up out of his chair, stepped* (step in place) *into his bathing suit,* and *went running* (run in place) *down to the river.* Then Oliver *jumped* (one jump) *in the river* and *swam across* (move arms in swimming motion). He *climbed out on the river bank, shook off the water,* and *hugged himself to get warm.* Then he saw the beautiful pony watching him. "Hello pony," Oliver said. The pony walked over to Oliver and stood patiently while Oliver *climbed on her back.* They had a wonderful time together, riding about in the meadow all that day. Oliver was so tired when he got home, he *sat in his chair* and *went to sleep.*

The end.

Sandra Peyser Hazouri and Miriam Smith McLaughlin

Activity 57

# Oliver Crumpet for Adults

**Time:**

3 minutes

**Number of People:**

Unlimited

**Materials/Preparation:**

None

**To Begin:**

- Tell the participants to listen to the story of Oliver Crumpet and to do whatever Oliver does.

- As you read the story, act it out. The group will follow your lead.

**To End:**

Tell the group they did a good job and applaud them.

# Oliver Crumpet

Oliver Crumpet *got up out of his chair* one morning and *looked out the window,* while *shading his eyes with his hands.* He *looked left* and he *looked right.* Then he *looked straight across the river* and saw a beautiful woman. "OOO, AHHH."

He *waved at her with his right hand.* He *waved at her with his left hand.* He *waved at her with both hands.* He even *jumped up and down.* The beautiful woman did not see him.

So he *stepped* (step in place) *into his bathing suit, ran* (run in place) *to the river* and *swam across* (move arms in swimming motion). When he got to the other side, Oliver *shook the water off, hugged himself to get warm,* and *sat down.*

The beautiful woman smiled at him and walked away in the direction of Faraway Places. Oliver followed her and was never seen again.

However, rumor has it that Oliver lives on the banks of some other river with three little Olivettes—all of them very beautiful.

The end.

## Activity 58
# A Quick Trip

**Time:**

3 to 5 minutes

**Number of People:**

Unlimited

**Materials/Preparation:**

None

**To Begin:**

- Ask the participants to stand and join you in the motions as you read the following:

  "We had a chance to go mountain climbing in Colorado" (Step in place, lifting legs high and swinging arms. Keep going until all the participants have joined in.)

  "We had another chance to go swimming in Florida" (Move arms in swimming motion. Keep going until all the participants have joined in.)

  "But we decided to go to Hawaii and Hula!

  (Wiggle your hips in hula fashion. Keep going until all have joined in.)

**To End:**

Tell the participants you hope the activity gave them an energy boost.

Activity 59
# Weather Report

**Time:**

5 minutes

**Number of People:**

Unlimited

**Materials/Preparation:**

Weather list: CLOUDY, RAINY, SUNNY, BREEZY, SNOWY, FREEZING, STORMY

**To Begin:**

- Ask the participants to leave their seats and mingle with the other participants.
- Tell them you will call out a kind of weather and when they hear the weather report they are to act as if they are experiencing the weather.
- To practice, ask the participants to act as if the weather is HOT.
- Call out each weather report, allowing just a few moments for the participants to act out.

**To End:**

- Ask the participants to act out their own weather reports.
- Tell them to act cloudy, sunny, and so forth according to how they are feeling.
- Tell the participants you are happy to see the sun shining in some parts of the room.

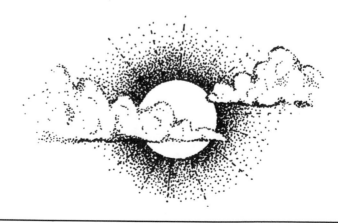

Sandra Peyser Hazouri and Miriam Smith McLaughlin

Activity 60

# Listen Carefully

**Time:**

5 minutes

**Number of People:**

Unlimited

**Materials/Preparation:**

None

**To Begin:**

- Tell the participants to listen carefully and follow the directions.
- Read "Listen Carefully" at a normal pace at first, increasing reading speed as you go.

**To End:**

- Ask who has a joke they are willing to share.

---

### Listen Carefully

Everyone stand, please. Everyone wearing green sit, please. If you are wearing black shoes, clap once. Everyone with brown hair stand, please. All black haired people please sit. If you are wearing white stand, please. Everyone with blue eyes wave, please. Everyone wearing red sit, please. If you have brown eyes please stand. Everyone wearing blue sit, please. If you are wearing uncomfortable shoes sit, please. If you were born in December, stand please. If you are happy, shake your right hand please. If you are wearing rings please sit. If you are very smart please stand. If you are wearing yellow clap, please. If you know a good joke, call out ha, ha, please. If you have green eyes whistle, please. If you have red hair please sit and stamp your feet. If you are getting tired sit, please. Everyone stand, please. If you are glad this is over, clap please.

---

Activity 61
# Smile Catchers

**Time:**

5 minutes

**Number of People:**

Unlimited (large group)

**Materials/Preparation:**

None

**To Begin:**

- Tell the participants that at the signal they should get up and move about the room shaking hands (or high five-ing) with as many people as possible.

- The participants *cannot smile at all* during this process *until* someone smiles at them first.

- Once they "catch a smile," they can smile at everyone they meet from then on.

- The participants may return to their seats as soon as they think that everyone in the room is smiling.

- Begin the activity with a signal or "go."

- As the leader, it will be up to you to start the "smile." Join the participants moving around and shaking hands, discreetly smile at one person and step out of the activity.

**To End:**

- Tell the participants how long it took to pass a smile around the room.

Activity 62
# I'm Terrific

**Time:**

5 minutes

**Number of People:**

Unlimited

**Materials/Preparation:**

None

**To Begin:**

- Read the statements below aloud, pausing after each one.
- Instruct the participants to listen carefully and to stand up if the statement applies to them.
- Instruct the participants to remain standing, sitting down only when they hear a statement that does not apply to them.

---

## Statements

I wish I had a million dollars.... I am older than I look.... I am younger than I look.... I would like to run for President.... Eating is one of my hobbies.... I am not afraid of anything.... I love my work.... I am not sure why I'm here.... I'm in love.... Brains run in my family.... I'm in great shape.... I am a terrific person (end with this statement).

---

**To End:**

- Ask the participants what they noticed about similarities and differences in the group.
- If someone stood alone, applaud that person for bravery.

---

Activity 63

# Five Minute Warning

**Time:**

5 minutes

**Number of People:**

Unlimited

**Materials/Preparation:**

Variety of music tapes, tape player.

**To Begin:**

- About five minutes before the start of the training/workshop, begin playing music loud enough to be heard throughout the room.

- At the beginning of the training/workshop, turn off the music and explain that you will be playing music at the end of each break.

- The music will start five minutes before the training/workshop begins, giving the participants that time to get back to their seats and be ready to work.

**To End:**

- At the end of the first break, compliment the group on their response to the music.

Activity 64

# How Does Your Garden Grow?

**Time:**

5 minutes

**Number of People:**

Unlimited

**Materials/Preparation:**

None

**To Begin:**

- Tell the participants to think of themselves as beautiful flowers growing in a garden. The flowers will grow to the following directions:
- Stand straight and tall but stay rooted right where you are.
- Bloom by lifting your arms up and out like petals.
- Sway in the breeze, arms held high.
- A hard rain is causing your petals to droop and the stems to slump over.
- The sun is out again and you can stand straight and bloom once more.
- Sway gently in the breeze once again.
- Tell the participants to be seated.

**To End:**

- Ask the participants how human beings are like flowers.

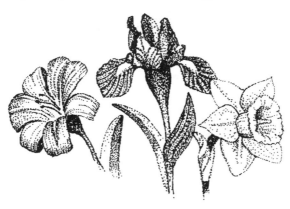

Activity 65
# Lazy Man's Aerobics

**Time:**

5 minutes

**Number of Participants:**

Unlimited

**Materials/Preparation:**

None

**To Begin:**

- Tell the participants to follow the instructions while remaining seated.
    1. Slowly rotate your head in a circle, reverse, rotate your head in opposite direction.
    2. Put your arms out to your side, clap your hands over your head, repeat and drop your arms.
    3. Lift your right arm, make a circle, and drop. Lift your left arm, make a circle, and drop.
    4. Lift both of your arms, make a circle, drop your arms to your side and shake out.
    5. Lift your feet off the floor and extend your legs. Repeat.
    6. Extend your right leg and make a circle. Extend your left leg and make a circle.
    7. Bend over at the waist, putting your head on your knees.

**To End:**

- Ask the participants to stand and stretch.

### Activity 66
# Balloon Ball I

**Time:**

5 to 8 minutes

**Number of People:**

Unlimited (divided into small groups)

**Materials/Preparation:**

Inflated balloons, one per group.

**To Begin:**

- Instruct the groups to stand in circles.

- On "go," the group members are to toss their balloons in the air and keep them elevated, using only their heads and bodies, no hands.

- If the balloon hits the floor, the group is out and must sit down.

**To End:**

- Recognize the group or groups that kept their balloons up for the longest time.

### Activity 67
# Balloon Ball II

**Time:**

5 to 8 minutes

**Number of People:**

Unlimited (divided into small groups)

**Materials/Preparation:**

Inflated balloons, one for each group.

**To Begin:**

- Instruct the groups to lay on the floor in circles, with their heads toward the center of the circles.
- On the word "go," they are to toss their balloons in the air and keep them elevated without using their hands or arms; bodies, feet, and heads are acceptable.
- If the balloon hits the floor, the group is out and must sit up.

**To End:**

- Recognize the group or groups that kept their balloon up for the longest time.

Activity 68
# Kick the Can't

**Time:**

5 to 15 minutes

**Number of People:**

Unlimited

**Materials/Preparation:**

Small pieces of paper, trash can

**To Begin:**

- Give each person a piece of paper and instruct them to write down something they think they can't do.
- Place the trash can in the center of the room. Instruct the participants to put their can't dos in the trash can and give the can a good kick.... That is, kick the can't.
- Tell the participants to say to themselves, "I can do it."
- Ask the group to say together, "I can do it."
- Ask the group to say it louder.
- Lead the group in applause.

**To End:**

- Ask for volunteers to share a time when they thought they couldn't do it and then found out they could.

Activity *69*
# Nap Time

**Time:**

5 to 15 minutes

**Number of People:**

Unlimited

**Materials/Preparation:**

Musical tape and tape player

**To Begin:**

- Some time in the afternoon, turn the lights low and close the shades.
- Play the music softly. Use a slow relaxing kind of music for this activity.
- Suggest to the participants that they get comfortable and close their eyes. They may lay their heads down on their desks if they wish.
- Encourage the group to take a few minutes nap.
- At the end of 2 to 15 minutes turn up the lights and turn off the music.

**To End:**

- Ask the participants to gently awaken neighbors who are still napping. Ask how the participants feel after their naps.

## Activity 70
# Line Dancing

**Time:**

8 to 10 minutes

**Number of People:**

Unlimited

**Materials/Preparation:**

Lively music tape, tape player, any additions leader may wish to add to the "dance."

**To Begin:**

- The leader or trainer should participate in and lead and call this activity.
- Call out all instructions.
- With the participants, form a circle and join hands.
- In rhythm to the music, begin by taking four steps right and then four steps left.
- Repeat.
- Walk in rhythm toward the center of the circle and hold joined hands up so they touch in the center.
- Step back in rhythm to a circle again.
- Drop hands and turn to the right. Hold the waist of the person in front.
- The leader steps out of the circle and leads the line around the room to the rhythm of the music as follows: Walk walk walk kick left Walk walk walk kick right
- The leader leads the line back into the circle and tells everyone to join hands once again.
- The circle comes together in the center again, with joined hands held up and gives a big "whoop."
- Group walks backward to form a circle again and leader says 'lets give it our all this time'.
- Group goes to the center again, joined hands held up and gives a big "whoop."

**To End:**

- Everyone applauds.

---

Activity 71

# Name that Word

**Time:**

8 to 10 minutes

**Number of People:**

Unlimited

**Materials/Preparation:**

Index cards, one for each participant. Print key words on index cards from the material the participants have used to this point in the workshop. Key words may be used more than once.

**To Begin:**

- Have the participants find a partner.
- Distribute index cards to each participant, making sure partners do not have the same word.
- The participants will have two minutes to talk to their partners about the word on their card without mentioning the word.
- The listening partner is to guess the word at the end of the two minutes.
- Give the participants a minute to think about what they will say.
- Decide which partner will talk first and begin.
- At the end of two minutes, reverse the roles and begin again.

**To End:**

- Ask the participants how it went.
- Ask them if they learned more being the speaking or the listening partner.

Activity 72
# The Fast Track

**Time:**

10 minutes

**Number of People:**

Unlimited

**Materials/Preparation:**

Timer or watch with second hand.

**To Begin:**

- Ask the participants to form a circle around the room.
- You will start an imaginary race car around the circle.
- As the race car gets to each participant, they are to say zoom.
- You will time how long it takes for the car to get back to you.
- Do a timed practice round by saying zoom and looking toward the person on your left. That should be repeated all the way around the circle until the person on your right "zooms" to you.
- Tell the participants how long the practice round took and encourage them to speed up.
- Start the "zoom" again to your left. Be sure to time it.
- Tell the participants that this is their last chance to beat their time.

**To End:**

- Tell the participants they set a record.
- Applaud each other.

Activity 73
# A Breath of Fresh Air

**Time:**

10 minutes

**Number of People:**

Unlimited

**Materials/Preparation:**

Background music tape and player (optional).

**To Begin:**

- Instruct the participants to get into comfortable positions in their chairs.
- Turn down the lights and play the music softly.
- Read the following vignette slowly and in a soft voice.

**To End:**

- Turn up the lights.
- Turn off the music.
- Ask the participants how they are feeling.
- Ask the participants if they enjoyed their brief escape.

# A Breath of Fresh Air

Relax (pause). Close your eyes (pause). Just relax (pause). Your body is beginning to feel comfortably heavy (pause). You are feeling more and more relaxed (pause). You are imagining yourself stretched out on a softly cushioned lounge chair (pause). Your body sinks into the cushions of the chair (pause). You are feeling peaceful and relaxed (pause).

You are stretched out on your cushioned chair on the deck of a huge glistening white ship (pause). The ship is not moving (pause). You feel safe and relaxed (pause). The ship is surrounded by a harbor of sparkling blue water (pause). You feel completely safe and peaceful (pause).

The only sounds you hear are the gentle lapping of the water against the ship and very far away, the rhythmic ringing of an ocean buoy (pause). You feel completely safe and peaceful (pause). Sunlight dances on the water of the harbor and feels slightly warm on your body (pause).

A gentle breeze moves the ships flag and brushes lightly across your face (pause). You feel completely safe and completely relaxed (pause). You smell the air. It smells fresh and clean (pause). You breathe deeply and sink still further into the soft cushions of your chair (long pause).

Gradually you begin to stir. You stretch out your legs (pause) and then your arms (pause). You open your eyes for a moment and then close them again (pause). You begin to become aware of your surroundings (pause). You have left the ship, and you are sitting in a room (pause). Other people are sitting around you (pause). You open your eyes (pause).

Welcome back.

Activity 74
# People Tricks

**Time:**

10 minutes

**Number of People:**

2 to 30

**Materials/Preparation:**

None

**To Begin:**

- Tell the group that most of us have a trick we can do or a noise or face we can make that we brought with us from our past.
- Give examples such as, "My brother can bend his little finger all the way back" or "I can quack like a duck."
- Instruct the group to think for a moment about tricks they can do or used to do in the past.
- Ask for volunteers to demonstrate their people tricks for the group.
- Applaud all efforts.

**To End:**

- Ask the participants how they felt doing this activity.
- Ask the participants for other ways they act "playful."

Activity 75
# A Silver Lining

**Time:**

10 minutes

**Number of People:**

Unlimited (divided into small groups)

**Materials/Preparation:**

None

**To Begin:**

- About half way through the workshop or class, invite the participants to share in their small groups something they like, appreciate or are enjoying about their experience.

- Ask the small groups to share with the other participants some of the experiences their group members mentioned.

**To End:**

- Ask the participants if their own perspective about the experience changed or was enhanced by the sharing of others. The leader may want to share also.

Activity 76
# Confusion

**Time:**

10 to 15 minutes

**Number of People:**

Unlimited

**Materials/Preparation:**

Write the following list on the board or newsprint.

| KEY WORDS | INSTRUCTIONS |
| --- | --- |
| Giraffe | Bend over, hands clasped in front of you. |
| Elephant | Stand straight, hands clasped above your head. |
| Alone | Group together with other the participants. |
| Group | Move away from others. |
| Sit | Stand up where you are. |
| Stand | Sit down where you are. |
| Against the wall | Move to center of the room. |
| Center of Area | Move near a wall of the room. |

**To Begin:**

- Tell the participants you will be reading a story.
- They are to listen for the key words in the story and follow the instructions. Point out that the instructions are the opposite of what the key word suggests. For example, when they hear the key words "against the wall," they should move to the center of the room. If they hear the key word "elephant" they should clasp their hands over their heads like a giraffe.
- Read the story at a slow even pace.
- Read the story a second time at a much faster pace.
- Tell the participants that the rules have now changed, and this time they are to do exactly what the key word suggests instead of the opposite.
- Applaud the group.

## The Story of the Elephant and the Giraffe

There once was an elephant who had a giraffe as his best friend. Often the elephant would lean against the wall alone and sit, waiting for the giraffe. The elephant's friend liked to go to the center of an area of grass and stand with other giraffes. Meanwhile the patient elephant would lean against the wall and sit until the giraffe left the center of the area of grass to come over and lean against the wall and stand by his friend.

**To End:**

- Ask the group how it was to hear one word and do something entirely different.

- After you learned to do the opposite, were you able to return to normal commands?

Activity 77
# Safari

**Time:**

15 minutes

**Number of People:**

Unlimited

**Materials/Preparation:**

Slips of paper, one for each participant, camera (optional). Write the names Mike, Mavis, and Dennis on three slips of paper. Write the names of the animals on the list below on the remaining slips of paper, using the same animal names over again until all slips are used.

**Animal List:** monkey, lion, elephant, parrot, hyena, snake

**To Begin:**

- Distribute slips of paper, one to each participant.
- Tell the participants that they are going to be players in a short story of a photographic safari.
- Each time they hear their animal named in the story they are to stand up, make the appropriate animal sound, and sit back down. When they hear the word "jungle," everyone stands up, makes their "animal noise" and sits back down.
- The person who has the Mavis slip is to stand and say "hello" when her name is called. The person with the Mike slip should stand and say "hey there" when his name is called and the person with the Dennis slip should say "howdy." If they hear the words, "the Motleys," both Mavis and Mike should stand and speak and then sit back down.
- Read the first sentence as a practice.
- Read the story all the way through, allowing time for the characters to stand and make their noises.

**To End:**

- Take a picture of the group if you have a camera.
- Applaud the group.

# The Safari

Mavis and Mike Motley and their guide Dennis started out on a photographic safari in Africa. They were headed for the jungle. Mike was hoping to get pictures of the monkeys and the lions in the jungle. But Mavis came to the jungle to photograph hyenas and parrots. Dennis was hoping they would not see any snakes, but he knew the jungle was full of snakes.

Amazingly, the first thing the Motleys saw as they entered the jungle were the elephants. Suddenly a pride of lions appeared, just as Dennis was snapping a picture of Mike and Mavis with the elephants. The lions were everywhere in the jungle. Dennis and the Motleys tried to scare them away as the parrots and the monkeys watched from the trees in the jungle.

Finally, Dennis and the Motleys continued their journey getting lots of picture of hyenas. In fact, the hyenas outnumbered the lions and the monkeys. Mike got a few pictures of the elephants and Mavis got one of the parrots.

It was a great jungle safari, full of laughs thanks to the hyenas. And best of all they didn't see any snakes.

Activity 78

# Your Number's Up

**Time:**

15 to 20 minutes

**Number of People:**

Unlimited (divided into small groups)

**Materials/Preparation:**

One die for each group.

List the rules of the game on newsprint and post where all can see.

**Rules**

- Roll a 1—Recite your name, birthdate and favorite food before passing the die to the next roller.
- Roll a 2—Good roll—Pass the die on.
- Roll a 3—Get up, run around the circle, and sit down before passing the die to the next roller.
- Roll a 4—Good roll—Pass the die on.
- Roll a 5—Sing the first line of "Row, Row, Row Your Boat."
- Roll a 6—Start over. All previous scores are erased.

**To Begin:**

- Instruct the group to sit in a circle on the floor or around the table.
- Give each group a die.
- The object of the game is to be the first group to roll a total of 56.
- Read the list of rules aloud.
- Remind the groups that they should take turns rolling the die.
- Keep track of the first 3 groups to get to 56.

**To End:**

- Announce the top three groups and have them stand for applause.

## Activity 79
# Famous People

**Time:**

15 to 20 minutes

**Number of People:**

Unlimited

**Materials/Preparation:**

Slips of paper, bowl or bag.

**To Begin:**

- Divide the participants in half.

- Pass slips of paper to one half of the participants and instruct them to write the name of a famous person on their slip. It can be someone alive or dead and should be known to the general public.

- Have the participants put the slips in the bowl or bag, not telling anyone else what they wrote.

- Pass the bag to the other half of the participants and have each one draw a slip.

- The participants who wrote the slip are to find the participant who drew their famous person. They should do so by asking questions about the famous person. For example: a participant whose famous person was a former president might ask, "Have you ever run for public office?" They may not ask a direct question such as, "Are you President X?"

- After the participants have found each other, instruct them to share two things about themselves with their partner.

**To End:**

- Ask for volunteers to share some interesting facts they learned about the famous people making up the group.

## Activity 80
# Bolly Volley

**Time:**

15 to 25 minutes

**Number of People:**

6 to 40

**Materials/Preparation:**

Six to ten balloons in two different colors (use more balloons for larger groups), masking tape, timer, rules for the game posted on newsprint (optional).

**To Begin:**

- Lay a strip of tape down the center of an open area to represent a net.

   Identify boundaries of "courts" on either side of the "net."

- Divide the group into two teams and tell them to spread themselves out within the boundaries of their respective "courts."

- Distribute balloons (one color to each team) to the team members standing along the back boundaries on each side.

- The task will be for the teams to trade balloons.

- The balloons must be batted over the 'net' (taped line) to the receiving team. The receiving team must then bat the balloons to their back row. A point will be scored for every balloon received in the back row.

- Review the rules listed below.

- Ask for questions and then start the game.

**To End:**

- Call time after 10 minutes

- Applaud the winners.

- Ask the participants what kind of teamwork was necessary to play the game successfully.

# Bolly Volley Rules

- All balloons must be started in the air at once.
- Only batting with open hands is allowed. No holding, punching or throwing balloons.
- If a balloon hits the floor on the sending side, it must be sent back to the back row and started again.
- If a balloon hits the floor on the receiving side, it must be sent to the net and started again.
- If a balloon breaks, the breaking team loses a point.
- When time is called, any balloon that has not made it over the net to the receiving team means a loss of one point for the sending team.
- If a balloon has made it over the net but has not reached the back row, no point is given or deducted.

Activity 81
# A Picture is Worth a Thousand Words

**Time:**

20 to 25 minutes

**Number of People:**

2 to 30

**Materials/Preparation:**

Plain paper, magazines, scissors, and glue.

**To Begin:**

- Halfway through the workshop/class, distribute collage materials.
- Ask each participant to look through the magazines for pictures to represent feelings and thoughts he or she is having at this point in the training.
- Arrange and glue the pictures on the paper in a collage format.
- Ask for volunteers to share their collages with the rest of the group
- Post the collages.

**To End:**

- Discuss significant feelings that have emerged in the collage activity.
- Be sure to address any issue that has surfaced that may affect the rest of the workshop.
- This activity is especially good for long workshops and classes.

Activity 82

# Music, Music, Music

**Time:**

30 minutes

**Number of People:**

Unlimited

**Materials/Preparation:**

Newsprint or plain paper, markers.

Make signs designating a kind of music.

## Suggested Music Categories

| | |
|---|---|
| Folk | Classical |
| Jazz | Country |
| Rock/Roll | Ballad |
| Rap | Baroque |
| Blues | |

**To Begin:**

- Post the signs around the room and instruct the participants to stand under the sign which designates "their kind of music."

- Ask the groups under each sign to come up with a song or music from their category that they can sing or hum for the rest of the groups.

- If there is a very small group or only one person, who is unwilling to sing, ask them to talk about the music for two minutes.

- Allow six to seven minutes preparation and practice time.

**To End:**

- Invite each group to perform.
- Applaud all efforts.

# Training Notes

Records of the activities used with various groups and the effectiveness of the activities in particular are useful tools for the group leader or trainer in planning future workshops.

| Activity | Date/Group | Notes |
|----------|------------|-------|
|          |            |       |
|          |            |       |
|          |            |       |
|          |            |       |
|          |            |       |
|          |            |       |
|          |            |       |
|          |            |       |
|          |            |       |
|          |            |       |
|          |            |       |
|          |            |       |
|          |            |       |

# Chapter IV
# Closure Activities

# Introduction

Closure is important anytime a program involves interaction among attendees. In order to move forward, the participants must experience some ending to the time and energy they have spent in the training or workshop. Planned activity at the end of the training or workshop gives the participants the structure and guidance they need to accomplish this task. What kind of closure the trainer chooses is dependent on the length of time the participants have spent together, who the participants are and the goals of the training or workshop.

The amount of time the participants have been together, however, should be the primary consideration. The more involved people get in a workshop or training the more connected they become. Groups that are together for several days or a week or two form strong bonds. They not only bond to one another, but to the experience they are having as well. In order to separate comfortably from the group and the experience, the participants must be offered the opportunity to reflect and to say good-bye. For groups whose interaction has been minimal, however, or who have been together for just a few hours, something as simple as applauding each other may be sufficient.

As with all activities planned for a training or workshop, choice of closure should consider the participants. Physical capabilities, ability to articulate thoughts and ideas, backgrounds or professions, age, and sometimes even sex should influence activity choices.

Finally, it is helpful too, in planning closure for the leader or trainer to decide what is important for the participants to take away with them. Closures can serve to highlight and review information, empower the participants and reinforce team bonding. The choice of the closure is then, a reflection of the goals of the workshop or training.

Activity 83
# Quick Close

**Time:**

3 to 5 minutes

**Number of People:**

Unlimited

**Materials/Preparation:**

None

**To Begin:**

- Invite any presenters to stand with you at the front of the room.
- Tell the participants that one at a time they are to stand, say their names and remain standing.
- Begin with the people already standing by saying your own name and looking next at whoever is standing with you.
- When the entire room is standing, ask the participants to give themselves a big hand for a job well done.

Activity 84

# Bye Bye Everybody

**Time:**

3 to 5 minutes

**Number of People:**

Unlimited

**Materials/Preparation:**

None

**To Begin:**

- Tell the participants that it is time to say good-bye.
- You will be reading them a poem and they are to do as the poem instructs. Everybody will wave to each other and say Bye Bye along with the reader.

**To End:**

- Move to the door, open it and stand there, immediately upon reading the last phrase of the poem.

**Note:**   This closure is great for encouraging a group to exit quietly.

# Poem: Bye Bye Everybody

It's been great

But it's getting late

Bye Bye everybody *(wave at each other and say together)*
   Bye Bye.

Nod to someone

'Cause it's been fun

Bye Bye everybody *(wave at each other and say together)*
   Bye Bye.

Give your neighbor a smile

That will last a while

Bye Bye everybody *(wave at each other and say together)*
   Bye Bye.

Shake hands with a friend

'Cause it's time to end

Bye Bye everybody *(wave at each other and say together)*
   Bye Bye.

Now move real slow Cause it's time to go

Bye Bye everybody.

*(Say together)* Bye Bye.

Activity 85
# Shake On It

**Time:**

4 to 5 minutes

**Number of People:**

Unlimited

**Materials/Preparation:**

None

**To Begin:**

- Ask the participants to find a partner
- Tell the participants to think of one idea or activity that they will take home to their own setting and use.
- Instruct partners to take turns telling what they plan to use and how, and to shake on it.
- Explain to the participants that the handshakes are their contracts.

**To End:**

- Wish the participants good luck on fulfilling their contracts.

Sandra Peyser Hazouri and Miriam Smith McLaughlin

Activity 86
# Round-Up and Recycle

**Time:**

5 minutes

**Number of People:**

Unlimited

**Materials/Preparation:**

Music tape, tape player, waste basket, large paper bags.

**To Begin:**

- Ask all of the participants to stand.

- Explain that when the music starts, they are to pick up all reusable handouts and pencils, and following the leader put them on a desk or table in the front of the room.

- Continuing to follow the leader, they are to pass by their desks, pick up any recyclable bottles or cans and drop them in bags at the front of the room.

- Following the same routine they are to remove all other trash near their desks and passing by the can at the front of the room, drop it in.

- The leader should be the first person on the right in the front row. All the participants should follow in line to the music, row by row.

- When the participants have completed the process they should sit down.

**To End:**

- Ask for volunteers to take the trash outside.

- Have the group decide where to take the recyclable materials.

Activity 87
# Ready to Roll

**Time:**

5 to 8 minutes

**Number of People:**

Unlimited

**Materials/Preparation:**

Five cardboard or newsprint signs printed with the following:

I'M SATISFIED

I'M FULL OF NEW LEARNING

I'M READY TO ROLL

I'M OLDER AND WISER

I'M LOOKING FOR MORE

**To Begin:**

- Post the signs around the room.
- Ask the participants to choose the sign that best describes them and go and stand beneath it.
- Talk for a minute with others that are standing beneath the sign to find out why they chose it.

**To End:**

- Ask one or two participants under each sign to share with the rest of the group why they chose it.
- Recognize anyone who stood alone under a sign.
- Applaud all participants.

## Activity 88
# One Last Word

**Time:**

5 to 8 minutes

**Number of People:**

Unlimited

**Materials/Preparation:**

None

**To Begin:**

- Instruct the participants to form a circle.
- Ask the participants to think of a word that describes how they are feeling at the end of the workshop.
- Tell them that they will take turns saying that one last word around the circle.
- The leader begins the activity.

**To End:**

- Ask the participants what kinds of feelings they heard.
- Acknowledge some of the feelings you heard expressed in the circle.

Activity 89
# Good-bye Around the World

**Time:**

5 to 10 minutes

**Number of People:**

Unlimited

**Materials/Preparation:**

Slips of paper, bag or basket. Write the words for good-bye on individual slips of paper. Repeat the words as is necessary for each participant to receive a word. The leader may wish to add words of other nationalities represented in the class or workshop.

## Words for Good-bye

1. Do svidamiya        Russian
2. Ciao                Italian
3. Arrivederci         Italian
4. Auf wiedershen      German
5. Kwa her             Swahili
6. Adios               Spanish
7. Aloha               Hawaiian
8. Adieu               French
9. Au revoir           French
10. Selemat djalan     Malaysian
11. Farval             Swedish
12. Tidama             West African
13. Do widzeniak       Polish
14. Shalom             Hebrew
15. Konnichi-wa        Japanese
16. Dan da go yue      Native American (Cherokee)

**Note:** The words and phrases are not literal translations of the word "good-bye."

## To Begin:

- Tell the participants to form a circle (if there is no room, the participants may stand at their desks).
- Place slips of paper in a basket and have each person draw one.
- The participants will each say their word in turn around the circle, doing the best they can with pronunciation. They are to join hands with the person next to them, as soon as that person has said his good-bye word.
- After everyone has said their word and joined hands, ask the group to say good-bye together in their own language.

## To End:

- Drop hands and wave saying "Good-bye everyone."

Activity 90
# The Information Exchange

**Time:**

5 to 10 minutes

**Number of People:**

Unlimited

**Materials/Preparation:**

Newsprint, markers, tape, plain paper, pencils

**To Begin:**

- Prior to the last break of the session, post newsprint around the room.

- Instruct the participants to take time during the break to write their names, addresses and phone numbers on the newsprint or to tape business cards to the newsprint.

**To End:**

- Allow the participants 5 to 10 minutes at the close to copy the names and addresses they want for future reference.

## Activity 91
# Saying Good-bye

**Time:**

10 to 15 minutes

**Number of People:**

Unlimited

**Materials/Preparation:**

None

**To Begin:**

- Tell the participants that it is time to say good-bye.

- Form one large circle around the room and count off by 2s.

- Tell the ones to take two steps in so that they form an inner circle and tighten up both circles.

- Circle 2 should turn and face someone in circle one.

- As circle one stands in place, circle 2 will say good-bye to the person he or she is facing in a way that is comfortable.

- Circle 2 will then move to the right and say good-bye to the next person in circle one.

- Continue until circle 2's have been all the way around circle one's.

- Next, instruct circle ones to form their own separate circle, and circle twos to do the same.

- Ask for a volunteer to begin moving around his or her circle to the left saying good-bye to each person and returning to his place in the circle. The person to the left of the volunteer should follow, saying good-bye around the circle and returning to his place.

**To End:**

- Tell the participants you will stand by the door as they leave, so that you too will have an opportunity to say good-bye to each of them.

Activity 92
# Memories

**Time:**

10 to 15 minutes

**Number of People:**

Six to 50 (divided into small groups)

**Materials/Preparation:**

None

**To Begin:**

- Instruct small groups to come up with 4 to 6 living "snapshots" of memorable moments in the class or training.
- A snapshot should consist of group members posed in a way that depicts an event or a memorable moment in the training.
- Make sure all group members are included in at least one of the snapshots.
- Groups should choose a narrator and prepare to display their snapshots and explain them to other participants.
- Applaud all efforts.

**To End:**

- Ask the participants to sit very still.
- Pretend to take a picture of them.
- Tell them what positive things you will remember about the group.

Activity 93

# Putting It All Together

**Time:**

15 minutes

**Number of People:**

10 to 30

**Materials/Preparation:**

Large piece of poster board, magic markers.

Print the following in large letters across the poster board:

## WE WORKED WELL TOGETHER AS A GROUP

Cut the poster into 30 pieces to make a puzzle.

**To Begin:**

- Distribute the puzzle pieces, one to each participant.
- Place any unused pieces on a desk or table at the front of the room.
- The participants will put their puzzle pieces together to form a poster with a message.
- The participants can get another piece from the front table once their piece is placed.

**To End:**

- Ask the participants to read the message aloud in unison.
- Lead the participants in applause.

Activity 94

# Thank You Notes

**Time:**

15 to 20 minutes

**Number of People:**

4 to 30

**Materials/Preparation:**

Post it notes or paper and tape

**To Begin:**

- Distribute a number of post it notes to each participant.
- Instruct the participants to write messages of appreciation to other group members on their note paper.
- Tell the participants to stick each message on the person for whom it is intended.
- As leader, you may wish to write a message to each participant, to ensure that everyone receives a thank you note.

**To End:**

- Ask the participants if there is anything else they wish to say before the end of the day.

Activity 95
# Tied with a Bow

**Time:**

15 to 20 minutes

**Number of People:**

Unlimited (divided into small groups)

**Materials/Preparation:**

Small slips of paper, bag or bowl for each group.

**To Begin:**

- Instruct the participants to write their names on small slips of paper and place them in a bowl or bag in the center of the group.

- Tell the participants to draw a name and to think of a gift for the person whose name they drew.

- The gift should be related to a special or unique quality of that person.

- The group members should take turns telling the person whose name they drew what gift they would give him or her and why. For example: If the person whose name you drew is good at summing up what others say, You might say, "I appreciate the way you summed things up for our groups and I would like to give you a calculator."

**To End:**

- Ask for volunteers to share some of the unique gift ideas they heard in their groups.

Activity 96
# Don't Forget to Write

**Time:**

20 minutes

**Number of People:**

Unlimited

**Materials/Preparation:**

Newsprint, magic markers, tape

**To Begin:**

- Hang the newsprint up around the room, one sheet for every 10 people. Write the word "messages" at the top of the sheets. Place magic markers nearby.

- Instruct the participants to write whatever they wish on the newsprint. Suggest they consider sharing how they feel or a special appreciation for someone else. They may have a wish for the group or themselves, or a pleasant memory of the day to write about.

**To End:**

- Encourage the group to read all the messages before they leave.

Activity 97
# Closure and Evaluation

**Time:**

20 minutes

**Number of People:**

Unlimited (divided into small groups)

**Materials/Preparation:**

Copies of list below or one copy of list on newsprint.

**To Begin:**

- Distribute closure and evaluation sheets.
- The participants are to complete the sheets and share their answers in small groups.

**To End:**

- Ask for volunteers to share some of the answers they heard in their small groups.
- Collect the sheets.

## Closure and Evaluation

I learned that....

I was surprised that....

I was reminded....

I especially enjoyed....

Some things I wish had been different were....

I never knew....

I plan to change....

## Activity 98
# Give a Friend a Hand

**Time:**

20 minutes

**Number of People:**

4 to 30

**Materials/Preparation:**

Poster board, plain paper, markers, bowl or bag.

Write the names of all the participants on slips of paper and place in a bowl or bag.

**To Begin:**

- Tell the participants to draw a name from the bowl and keep it a secret.
- Instruct the participants to trace their open hands on poster board or paper. In the palm of the hand they will write the name of the person they picked.
- In each finger, they are to write a positive word or phrase about that person.
- One at a time, the participants will stand and share with the rest of the group, who they wrote about and what they said.

**To End:**

- After they have shared, the participants will give the hand they made to that person.

Activity 99
# Perfection

**Time:**

20 to 30 minutes

**Number of People:**

Unlimited (divided into small groups)

**Materials/Preparation:**

Newsprint, magic markers, crayons. Optional: colored paper, foil, decorative materials, scissors, tape, glue.

**To Begin:**

- Distribute one piece of newsprint and markers to each group.
- Ask the participants to reflect on what they have learned in the workshop or class.
- Work in groups to design perfection or the ideal related to the subject matter of the class or workshop. For example: If the participants are students, they could design the perfect school. If the participants are adults in a time management training, they could design an ideal day or a perfectly efficient office.
- There are no limits or constraints.
- After 10 minutes, invite groups to present their ideas of perfection to the other groups.
- Applaud all efforts.

**To End:**

- Ask the groups what things in their designs could reasonably be achieved.

Activity 100
# Building Bridges

**Time:**

20 to 30 minutes

**Number of People:**

Unlimited (divided into small groups)

**Materials/Preparation:**

Plain white paper, pens or pencils, markers.

**To Begin:**

- Distribute paper and pencils.
- Each one of the participants will "build" a bridge on paper.
- The bridge should show how the participant might incorporate what he or she has learned in this workshop/training into his or her work or life.
- Allow 10 to 12 minutes for the participants to work.
- Have the participants share their bridges in their groups.

**To End:**

- Ask groups to talk about some of the ideas that were shared.

Activity 101
# The Latest News

**Time:**

30 minutes

**Number of People:**

4 to 30 (divided into small groups)

**Materials/Preparation:**

Index cards, markers, newsprint. On individual index cards print the following:

Bugs Bunny and Company

Soap Opera

Newscast

Talk show

Situation Comedy

Game Show

**To Begin:**

- About halfway through the workshop or class or at the end of the workshop or class, distribute one index card to each small group.
- Tell the groups that they are to present a highlight or two from the workshop in the format described on the card. The presentation should be no more that three minutes.
- Allow groups 7 or 8 minutes of planning time.
- Have groups present and applaud all efforts.

**To End:**

- Ask for comments about the highlights that were chosen.

# Training Notes

Records of the activities used with various groups and the effectiveness of the activities in particular are useful tools for the group leader or trainer in planning future workshops.

| Activity | Date/Group | Notes |
|----------|-----------|-------|
| _____ | _____ | _____ |
| _____ | _____ | _____ |
| _____ | _____ | _____ |
| _____ | _____ | _____ |
| _____ | _____ | _____ |
| _____ | _____ | _____ |
| _____ | _____ | _____ |
| _____ | _____ | _____ |
| _____ | _____ | _____ |
| _____ | _____ | _____ |
| _____ | _____ | _____ |
| _____ | _____ | _____ |
| _____ | _____ | _____ |
| _____ | _____ | _____ |
| _____ | _____ | _____ |

Sandra Peyser Hazouri and Miriam Smith McLaughlin

# Bibliography

Fluegelman, A. (1976). *The new games book.* New York: Doubleday.

Fluegelman, A. (1981). *More new games!* New York: Doubleday.

Foster, E.S. (1989). *Energizers and icebreakers: For all ages and stages.* Minneapolis, MN: Educational Media Corporation.

Hazouri, S.P., & Smith, M.F. (1991). *Peer listening in the middle school: Training activities for students.* Minneapolis, MN: Educational Media Corporation.

McLaughlin, M.S., & Hazouri, S.P. (1992). *TLC •tutoring •leading •cooperating: Training activities for elementary school students.* Minneapolis, MN: Educational Media Corporation.

## About the Authors

**Miriam Smith McLaughlin** is the prevention training consultant for the State Department of Public Instruction in Raleigh, North Carolina. She is a state and national trainer for peer programming and a member of the Board of the North Carolina Peer Helper Association. Mrs. McLaughlin is the author of numerous educational articles, co-author of the nationally acclaimed parent training manual, *D.A.R.E. to Parent,* and co-author of *Peer Listening in the Middle School* and *TLC •Tutoring •Leading •Cooperating: Training Activities for Elementary School Students.* Mrs. McLaughlin is a native of Massachusetts. She currently resides in Raleigh, North Carolina.

**Sandra Peyser Hazouri** is a school counseling consultant for the State Department of Public Instruction in Raleigh, North Carolina. She has served as an elementary teacher, counselor, and peer program supervisor. She has contributed to the field of peer work by doing state and national training workshops and by serving as the President of the North Carolina Peer Helper Association. Ms. Hazouri is the co-author of *Peer Listening in the Middle School* and *TLC •Tutoring •Leading •Cooperating: Training Activities for Elementary School Students.* She is a native of Miami, Florida and resides in Raleigh, North Carolina with her children.